Episcopal Church

Additional Hymns Set Forth by the House of Bishops

at the request of the House of Clerical and Lay Deputies, in General

Convention, October, 1865

Episcopal Church

Additional Hymns Set Forth by the House of Bishops
at the request of the House of Clerical and Lay Deputies, in General Convention, October, 1865

ISBN/EAN: 9783337830069

Printed in Europe, USA, Canada, Australia, Japan

Cover: Foto ©Lupo / pixelio.de

More available books at **www.hansebooks.com**

ADDITIONAL HYMNS

SET FORTH BY THE

HOUSE OF BISHOPS,

AT THE REQUEST OF THE

HOUSE OF CLERICAL AND LAY DEPUTIES,

IN

GENERAL CONVENTION, OCTOBER, 1865;

TO BE USED IN THE CONGREGATIONS OF THE PROTESTANT
EPISCOPAL CHURCH IN THE UNITED
STATES OF AMERICA.

———◆———

PHILADELPHIA
J. B. LIPPINCOTT & CO.
1868.

ADDITIONAL HYMNS.

REDEMPTION.

Hymn 213.

II 4

BLOW ye the trumpet, blow;
The gladly-solemn sound!
Let all the nations know,
To earth's remotest bound,
The year of jubilee is come;
Return, ye ransomed sinners, home.

2 Jesus, our great High Priest,
Hath full atonement made:
Ye weary spirits, rest;
Ye mournful souls, be glad;
The year of jubilee is come;
Return, ye ransomed sinners, home.

3 Extol the Lamb of God,
The sin-atoning Lamb;
Redemption by his blood
Throughout the world proclaim:
The year of jubilee is come;
Return, ye ransomed sinners, home.

4 Ye slaves of sin and hell,
   Your liberty receive,
And safe in Jesus dwell,
   And blest in Jesus live:
The year of jubilee is come;
Return, ye ransomed sinners, home.

5 Ye who have sold for naught
   Your heritage above,
Receive it back unbought,
   The gift of Jesus' love:
The year of jubilee is come;
Return, ye ransomed sinners, home.

6 The gospel trumpet hear,
   The news of heavenly grace;
And, saved from earth, appear
   Before your Saviour's face:
The year of jubilee is come;
Return, ye ransomed sinners, home.

Hymn 214.   C. M.

THERE is a fountain filled with blood
   Drawn from Emmanuel's veins;
And sinners plunged beneath that flood
   Lose all their guilty stains.

2 The dying thief rejoiced to see
   That fountain in his day;
And there may I, as vile as he,
   Wash all my sins away.

3 Dear, dying Lamb, Thy precious blood
    Shall never lose its power,
Till all the ransomed church of God
    Be saved, to sin no more.

4 E'er since, by faith, I saw the stream
    Thy flowing wounds supply,
Redeeming love has been my theme,
    And shall be till I die.

5 Then in a nobler, sweeter song,
    I'll sing Thy power to save;
When this poor lisping, stammering tongue
    Lies silent in the grave.

THE CHURCH.

Hymn 215. III. 3.

GLORIOUS things of thee are spoken,
    Zion, city of our God:
He, whose word cannot be broken,
    Formed thee for his own abode;
On the rock of ages founded,
    What can shake thy sure repose?
With salvation's walls surrounded,
    Thou may'st smile at all thy foes.

2 See, the streams of living waters,
    Springing from eternal love,
Well supply thy sons and daughters,
    And all fear of want remove;

1 *

Who can faint while such a river
    Ever flows their thirst t' assuage?
Grace, which like the Lord, the Giver,
    Never fails from age to age.

3 Round each habitation hovering,
    See the cloud and fire appear,
For a glory and a covering,
    Showing that the Lord is near.
Blest inhabitants of Zion,
    Washed in the Redeemer's blood!
Jesus, whom their souls rely on,
    Makes them kings and priests to God.

4 Saviour, if of Zion's city
    I through grace a member am,
Let the world deride or pity,
    I will glory in Thy name:
Fading is the worldling's pleasure,
    All his boasted pomp and show;
Solid joys and lasting treasure,
    None but Zion's children know.

Hymn 216.   C. M.

COME, let us join our friends above,
    That have obtained the prize,
And on the eagle wings of love,
    To joys celestial rise:

2 Let all the saints terrestrial sing,
    With those to glory gone:
For all the servants of our King,
    In earth and heaven, are one.

3 One family, we dwell in Him;
  One church above, beneath;
Though now divided by the stream,—
  The narrow stream of death.

4 One army of the living God,
  To His command we bow;
Part of His host have crossed the flood,
  And part are crossing now.

5 Ten thousand to their endless home,
  This solemn moment fly;
And we are to the margin come,
  And we expect to die.

6 Then, Lord of Hosts, be Thou our Guide,
  And we, at Thy command,
Through waves that part on either side,
  Shall reach Thy blessed land.

Hymn 217. C. M.

THE Son of God goes forth to war,
  A kingly crown to gain;
His blood-red banner streams afar:
  Who follows in His train?

2 Who best can drink His cup of woe,
  And triumph over pain,
Who patient bear His cross below,
  He follows in His train.

3 The martyr first, whose eagle eye
    Could pierce beyond the grave,
Who saw his Master in the sky,
    And called on Him to save.

4 Like Him, with pardon on his tongue,
    In midst of mortal pain,
He prayed for them that did the wrong:
    Who follows in His train?

5 A glorious band, the chosen few,
    On whom the Spirit came:
Twelve valiant saints, their hope they knew,
    And mocked the cross and flame.

6 They met the tyrant's brandished steel,
    The lion's gory mane;
They bowed their necks the death to feel;
    Who follows in their train?

7 A noble army, men and boys,
    The matron and the maid,
Around the Saviour's throne rejoice,
    In robes of light arrayed.

8 They climbed the dizzy steep of heaven,
    Through peril, toil, and pain;
Oh God! to us may grace be given
    To follow in their train!

ADVENT.

Hymn 218. III. 3.

HARK! a thrilling voice is sounding;
 "Christ is nigh!" it seems to say,
"Cast away the works of darkness,
 O ye children of the day!"

2 Wakened by the solemn warning,
 Let the earth-bound soul arise;
Christ, our Sun, all sloth dispelling,
 Rises in the morning skies.

3 Lo! the Lamb, so long expected,
 Comes with pardon down from heaven·
Let us haste, in godly sorrow,
 Through His blood to be forgiven.

4 So when next He comes with glory,
 Wrapping all the earth in fear,
May we by His love be shielded!
 May He to forgive draw near!

Hymn 219. III. 3

SEE, He comes! whom every nation,
 Taught of God, desired to see,
Filled with hope and expectation
 That He would their Saviour be.

Sing! oh sing, with exultation!
Haste we to our Father's home!
Peace, redemption, joy, salvation,
Now from heaven to earth are come!

2 See, He comes! whom kings and sages,
. Prophets, patriarchs of old,
Distant climes, and countless ages,
Waited eager to behold.
Sing! oh sing with exultation!
Haste we to our Father's home!
Peace, redemption, joy, salvation,
Now from heaven to earth are come!

3 See! the Lamb of God appearing!
God of God, from heaven above!
See the heavenly Bridegroom cheering
His own Bride with words of love!
Glory to the Eternal Father,
Glory to the Incarnate Son,
Glory to the Holy Spirit,
Glory to the Three in One!

Hymn 220.   C. M

NOW gird your patient loins again,
Your wasting torches trim!
The chief of all the sons of men,
Who will not welcome Him?

2 Rejoice, the hour is near! At length
The Journeyer, on His way,
Comes in the greatness of His strength,
To keep His festal day.

3 Oh let the streams of solemn thought
  Which in His temples rise,
From deeper sources spring, than aught
  Born of the changing skies.

4 Then, though the summer's pride departs,
  And winter's withering chill
Rests on the cheerless woods, our hearts
  Shall be unchanging still.

Hymn 221. C. M.

ONCE more, O Lord, Thy sign shall be
  Upon the heavens displayed,
And earth and its inhabitants
  Be terribly afraid:
For, not in weakness clad, Thou com'st,
  Our woes, our sins to bear,
But girt with all Thy Father's might,
  His judgment to declare.

2 The terrors of that awful day,
  Oh! who can understand?
Or who abide, when Thou in wrath
  Shalt lift Thy holy hand?
The earth shall quake, the sea shall roar
  The sun in heaven grow pale;
But Thou hast sworn, and wilt not change,
  Thy faithful shall not fail.

3 Then grant us, Saviour, so to pass
  Our time in trembling here,
That when upon the clouds of heaven
  Thy glory shall appear,

Uplifting high our joyful heads,
    In triumph we may rise,
And enter, with Thine angel train,
    Thy palace in the skies.

Hymn 222.   L M

HOSANNA to the living Lord!
    Hosanna to th' incarnate Word!
To Christ, Creator, Saviour, King,
Let earth, let heaven, hosanna sing.

2 Hosanna, Lord! Thine angels cry;
Hosanna, Lord!. Thy saints reply.
Above, beneath us, and around,
The dead and living swell the sound.

3 O Saviour! with protecting care,
Return to this, Thy house of prayer:
Assembled in Thy sacred name,
Here we Thy parting promise claim.

4 But chiefest in our cleansed breast,
Eternal! bid Thy Spirit rest;
And make our secret soul to be
A temple pure, and worthy Thee.

5 So, in the last and dreadful day,
When earth and heaven shall melt away,
Thy flock, redeemed from sinful stain,
Shall swell the sound of praise again.

CHRISTMAS.

Hymn 223.   III. 3.

HARK! what mean those holy voices,
   Sweetly sounding through the skies?
Lo! th' angelic host rejoices;
   Heavenly hallelujahs rise.

2 Cherubs tell the wondrous story,
   Joyous seraphim reply,
"Glory in the highest, glory!
   Glory be to God most high!

3 Peace on earth, good-will from Heaven,
   Reaching far as man is found;
Souls redeemed, and sins forgiven!
   Loud our grateful harps shall sound.

4 Christ is born, the great Anointed;
   Heaven and earth His praises sing!
Oh receive whom God appointed,
   For your Prophet, Priest, and King!

5 Hasten, mortals, to adore Him;
   Learn His name to magnify,
Till in heaven ye sing before Him,
   Glory be to God most high!"

2

NEW YEAR.

Hymn 224.   III. 1.

WHILE with ceaseless course the sun
   Hasted through the former year,
Many souls their race have run,
   Never more to meet us here:
Fixed·in an eternal state,
   They have done with all below:
We a little longer wait,
   But how little, none can know.

2 As the winged arrow flies
   Speedily the mark to find;
As the lightning from the skies
   Darts, and leaves no trace behind,
Swiftly thus our fleeting days
   Bear us down life's rapid stream;
Upward, Lord, our spirits raise;
   All below is but a dream.

3 Thanks for mercies past receive;
   Pardon of our sins renew;
Teach us henceforth how to live
   With eternity in view:
Bless Thy word to young and old;
   Fill us with a Saviour's love;
And when life's short tale is told, ·
   May we dwel with Thee above.

EPIPHANY.

Hymn 225. P. M.

BRIGHTEST and best of the sons of the
morning!
 Dawn on our darkness, and lend us Thine
  aid!
Star of the East, the horizon adorning,
 Guide where our infant Redeemer is laid.

2 Cold on His cradle the dew-drops are
  shining;
 Low lies His head with the beasts of the
  stall:
Angels adore Him in slumber reclining,
 Maker, and Monarch, and Saviour of all.

3 Say, shall we yield Him, in costly devotion,
 Odors of Edom, and offerings divine,
Gems of the mountain, and pearls of the
  ocean,
 Myrrh from the forest, and gold from the
  mine?

4 Vainly we offer each ample oblation,
 Vainly with gifts would His favor se-
  cure;
Richer, by far, is the heart's adoration,
 Dearer to God are the prayers of the
  poor.

5 Brightest and best of the sons of the
    morning!
  Dawn on our darkness, and lend us Thine
    aid!
  Star of the East, the horizon adorning,
    Guide where our infant Redeemer is laid.

LENT.

Hymn 226.   P. M.

JESUS, let Thy pitying eye
  Call back a wandering sheep:
Prone, like Peter, to deny,
  Like Peter, I would weep.
Let me be by grace restored;
  On me be all long-suffering shown;
Turn, and look upon me, Lord,
  And break my heart of stone.

2 Saviour, Prince, enthroned above,
  Repentance to impart,
Give me, through Thy dying love,
  The humble, contrite heart;
Give what I have long implored,
  A portion of Thy grief unknown;
Turn, and look upon me, Lord,
  And break my heart of stone.

3 For Thine own compassion's sake
  The gracious wonder show;

Cast my sins behind Thy back,
And wash me white as snow:
Let Thy pity help afford,
And while I do myself bemoan,
Turn, and look upon me, Lord,
And break my heart of stone.

Hymn 227.   L M

MY dear Redeemer and my Lord,
I read my duty in Thy word;
But in Thy life the law appears,
Drawn out in living characters.

2 Such was Thy truth and such Thy zeal.
Such deference to Thy Father's will,
Such love, and meekness so d'vine,
I would transcribe and make them mine.

3 Cold mountains and the midnight air
Witnessed the fervor of Thy prayer;
The desert Thy temptations knew,
Thy conflict, and Thy victory too.

4 Be Thou my pattern, make me bear
More of Thy gracious image here;
Then God the Judge shall own my name
Among the followers of the Lamb.

2 *   B

PASSION WEEK.

Hymn 228.   C. M

ALAS! and did my Saviour bleed?
  And did my Sovereign die?
Would He devote that sacred head
For such a worm as I?

2 Was it for crimes that I have done
    He groaned upon the tree?
Amazing pity! grace unknown!
  And love beyond degree!

3 Well might the sun in darkness hide,
    And shut his glories in,
When God, the mighty Maker, died,
  For man, the creature's sin.

4 Thus might I hide my blushing face,
    While His dear cross appears,
Dissolve my heart in thankfulness,
  And melt mine eyes in tears.

5 But drops of grief can ne'er repay
    The debt of love I owe:
Here, Lord, I give myself away,
  'Tis all that I can do.

Hymn 229.   III 3.

HAIL, Thou once despised Jesus,
  Hail, Thou Galilean King;
Thou didst suffer to release us;
  Thou didst free salvation bring!
Hail, Thou agonizing Saviour,
  Bearer of our sin and shame;
By Thy merit find we favor;
  Life is given through Thy name.

2 Paschal Lamb, by God appointed,
    All our sins on Thee were laid;
  By almighty love anointed,
    Thou hast full atonement made.
  All Thy people are forgiven,
    Through the virtue of Thy blood,
  Opened is the gate of heaven,
    Man is reconciled to God.

3 Jesus, low we bow before Thee,
    Mediator glorified!
  All the heavenly hosts adore Thee,
    Seated at Thy Father's side;
  There for sinners Thou art pleading,
    There Thou dost our place prepare;
  Ever for us interceding,
    Till in glory we appear.

4 Worship, honor, power, and blessing
    Thou art worthy to receive;
  Loudest praises, never ceasing,
    Meet it is for us to give.

Help, ye bright angelic spirits,
   Bring your sweetest, noblest lays;
Help to sing our Saviour's merits,
   Help to chant Emmanuel's praise.

GOOD FRIDAY.

Hymn 230.   III. 2.

GO to dark Gethsemane,
   Ye that feel the tempter's power,
Your Redeemer's conflict see,
   Watch with Him one bitter hour;
Turn not from His griefs away,
Learn of Jesus Christ to pray.

2 Follow to the judgment hall;
   View the Lord of life arraigned;
Oh, the wormwood and the gall;
   Oh, the pangs His soul sustained!
Shun not suffering, shame, or loss;
Learn of Him to bear the cross.

3 Calvary's mournful mountain climb;
   There, adoring at His feet,
Mark the miracle of time,
   God's own sacrifice complete;
"It is finished!"—hear Him cry;
Learn of Jesus Christ to die.

Hymn 231.

II. 6.

OH, sacred head, now wounded!
  With grief and shame weighed down!
Oh, sacred brow, surrounded
  With thorns, Thy only crown!
Oh, sacred head, what glory,
  What bliss, till now was Thine!
Yet though despised and gory,
  I joy to call Thee mine.

2 On me, as Thou art dying,
  Oh turn Thy pitying eye!
To Thee for mercy crying,
  Before Thy cross I lie.
Thy grief and Thy compassion
  Were all for sinners' gain;
Mine, mine was the transgression,
  But Thine the deadly pain.

3 What language shall I borrow
  To praise Thee, dearest Friend,
For this, Thy dying sorrow,
  Thy pity without end!
Oh, make me Thine for ever,
  And should I fainting be,
Lord, let me never, never,
  Outlive my love to Thee.

4 Be near when I am dying;
  Oh, show Thy cross to me!
And to my succor flying,
  Come, Lord, and set me free.

These eyes new faith receiving,
   From Thine eyes shall not move;
For he who dies believing
   Dies safely through Thy love.

Hymn 232.   II. 4

THE atoning work is done,
   The Victim's blood is shed,
And Jesus now is gone
   His people's cause to plead;
He stands in heaven their great High Priest,
And bears their names upon His breast.

2 He sprinkles with His blood
   The mercy-seat above;
For justice had withstood
   The purposes of love;
But justice now withstands no more,
And mercy yields her boundless store.

3 No temple made with hands,
   His place of service is;
In heaven itself He stands;
   A Heavenly Priesthood His.
In Him the shadows of the law
Are all fulfilled, and now withdraw.

4 And though awhile He be
   Hid from the eyes of men,
His people look to see
   Their great High Priest again;
In brightest glory He will come,
And take His waiting people home.

EASTER.

Hymn 233. .II. 1

JESUS Christ is risen to-day,
  Our triumphant holiday;
Who did once upon the cross
Suffer to redeem our loss.
                    Hallelujah!

2 Hymns of praise then let us sing
Unto Christ, our heavenly King;
Who endured the cross and grave,
Sinners to redeem and save.
                    Hallelujah!

3 But the pains which He endured
Our salvation have procured;
Now above the sky He's King,
Where the angels ever sing,
                    Hallelujah!

ASCENSION.

Hymn 234. III 1.

HAIL the day that sees Him rise,
  Glorious, to His native skies!
Christ, awhile to mortals given,
Enters now the highest heaven.

2 There for Him high triumph waits;
Lift your heads, eternal gates!
Conqueror over death and sin,
Take the King of glory in.

3 Lo, the heaven its Lord receives!
Yet He loves the earth He leaves:
Though returning to His throne,
Still He calls mankind His own.

4 Still for us He intercedes,
His prevailing death He pleads;
Near Himself prepares our place,
Great Forerunner of our race.

5 Lord, though parted from our sight,
Far above yon azure height,
Grant our hearts may thither rise
Following Thee beyond the skies.

6 Master (will we ever say,)
Taken from our head to-day,
See Thy faithful servants, see,
Ever gazing up to Thee.

Hymn 235. L. M.

WHERE high the heavenly temple
stands,
The house of God not made with hands,
A great High-Priest our nature wears,
The guardian of mankind appears.

2 Though now ascended up on high,
He bends to earth a brother's eye;
Partaker of the human name,
He knows the frailty of our frame.

3 Our fellow-sufferer yet retains,
A fellow-feeling for our pains;
And still remembers, in the skies,
His tears, His agonies, and cries.

4 In every pang that rends the heart,
The Man of sorrows had a part;
He sympathizes in our grief,
And to the sufferer sends relief.

5 With boldness, therefore, at the throne,
Let us make all our sorrows known,
And ask the aids of heavenly power,
To help us in the evil hour.

WHITSUNDAY.

Hymn 236.   L. M

CREATOR Spirit! by whose aid
The world's foundations first were laid,
Come, visit every waiting mind;
Come, pour Thy joys on human kind.

2 Thrice Holy Fount, thrice Holy Fire,
Our hearts with heavenly love inspire;
Come, and Thy sacred unction bring
To sanctify us while we sing.

3

3 O Source of uncreated light,
   The Father's promised Paraclete!
   From sin and sorrow set us free,
   And make us temples worthy Thee!

4 Our frailties help, our vice control,
   Subdue the senses to the soul;
   And when rebellious they are grown,
   Then lay Thy hand and hold them down.

5 Chase from our minds th' infernal foe,
   And peace, the fruit of love, bestow;
   And lest our feet should step astray,
   Protect and guide us in the way.

6 Make us eternal truths receive,
   And practice all that we believe;
   Give us Thyself, that we may see
   The Father and the Son, by Thee.

Hymn 237.   S. M.

LORD God, the Holy Ghost,
     In this accepted hour,
As on the day of Pentecost,
   Descend in all Thy power;
We meet with one accord
   In our appointed place,
And wait the promise of our Lord,
   The Spirit of all grace.

2 Like mighty, rushing wind
     Upon the waves beneath,
Move with one impulse every mind,
   One soul, one feeling breathe:

The young, the old inspire
  With wisdom from above;
And give us hearts and tongues of fire
  To pray, and praise, and love.

3 Spirit of Light, explore,
  And chase our gloom away,
With lustre shining more and more
  Unto the perfect day:
Spirit of Truth be Thou
  In life and death our guide;
O Spirit of Adoption, now
  May we be sanctified.

Hymn 238.   C. M

SPIRIT of Truth! on this Thy day
  To Thee for help we cry,
To guide us through the dreary way
  Of dark mortality.

2 We ask not, Lord, the cloven flame
  Or tongues of various tone;
But long Thy praises to proclaim,
  With fervor in our own.

3 We mourn not that prophetic skill
  Is found on earth no more;
Enough for us to trace Thy will
  In Scripture's sacred lore.

4 Though tongues shall cease and power decay,
  And knowledge empty prove,
Do Thou Thy trembling servants stay
  With faith, with hope, with love.

TRINITY SUNDAY.

Hymn 239. III. 5.

HOLY Father, great Creator,
  Source of mercy, love, and peace,
Look upon the Mediator,
  Clothe us with His righteousness;
    Heavenly Father,
  Through the Saviour, hear and bless.

2 Holy Jesus, Lord of Glory,
  Whom angelic hosts proclaim,
While we hear Thy wondrous story,
  Meet and worship in Thy name,
    Dear Redeemer,
  In our hearts Thy peace proclaim.

3 Holy Spirit, Sanctifier,
  Come with unction from above,
Raise our hearts to raptures higher,
  Fill them with the Saviour's love!
    Source of comfort,
  Cheer us with the Saviour's love.

4 God the Lord, through every nation
  Let Thy wondrous mercies shine!
In the song of Thy salvation
  Every tongue and race combine!
    Great Jehovah,
  Form our hearts and make them Thine.

Hymn 240. P. M

THOU, whose Almighty word
Chaos and darkness heard,
And took their flight!
Hear us, we humbly pray.
And where the gospel day
Sheds not its glorious ray,
Let there be light!

2 Thou who didst come to bring
On Thy redeeming wing
Healing and sight,
Health to the sick in mind,
Light to the spirit-blind,
Oh, now to all mankind
Let there be light!

3 Spirit of Truth and Love,
Life-giving, holy Dove,
Speed forth Thy flight!
Move on the water's face,
Spreading the beams of grace,
And in earth's darkest place
Let there be light!

4 Blessed and Holy Three,
Glorious Trinity,
Grace, Love, and Light!
Through the world, far and wide,
Boundless as ocean's tide
Rolling in fullest pride,
Let there be light!

3 *

THANKSGIVING DAY.

Hymn 241.   L. M.

GREAT God, as seasons disappear,
And changes mark the rolling year;
As time with rapid pinions flies,
May every season make us wise.

2 Long has Thy favor crowned our days,
And summer shed again its rays;
No deadly cloud our sky has veiled;
No blasting winds our path assailed.

3 Our harvest months have o'er us rolled,
And filled our fields with waving gold;
Our tables spread, our garners stored!
Where are our hearts to praise the Lord?

4 The solemn harvest comes apace,
The closing day of life and grace;
Time of decision, awful hour!
Around it let no tempests lower!

5 Prepare us, Lord, by grace divine,
Like stars in heaven to rise and shine;
Then shall our happy souls above
Reap the full harvest of Thy love!

Hymn 242.   II. 4

BEFORE the Lord we bow,
  The God who reigns above,
And rules the world below,
  Boundless in power and love.
    Our thanks we bring
    In joy and praise,
    Our hearts we raise
  To heaven's high King.

2 The nation Thou hast blest
  May well Thy love declare,
From foes and fears at rest,
  Protected by Thy care.
    For this fair land,
    For this bright day,
    Our thanks we pay—
  Gifts of Thy hand.

3 May every mountain height,
  Each vale and forest green,
Shine in Thy word's pure light,
  And its rich fruits be seen!
    May every tongue
    Be tuned to praise,
    And join to raise
  A grateful song.

4 Earth! hear thy Maker's voice,
  The great Redeemer own,
Believe, obey, rejoice,
  And worship Him alone;

Cast down thy pride,
Thy sin deplore,
And bow before
The Crucified.

5 And when in power He comes,
Oh, may our native land,
From all its rending tombs,
Send forth a glorious band;
A countless throng
Ever to sing
To heaven's high King
Salvation's song.

CONFIRMATION.

Hymn 243.

MY faith looks up to Thee,
Thou Lamb of Calvary,
Saviour divine!
Now hear me while I pray:
Take all my guilt away;
Oh, let me from this day
Be wholly Thine.

2 May Thy rich grace impart
Strength to my fainting heart;
My zeal inspire;

As Thou hast died for me,
Oh, may my love to Thee
Pure, warm, and changeless be,
  A living fire.

3 While life's dark maze I tread,
And griefs around me spread,
  Be Thou my guide;
Bid darkness turn to day;
Wipe sorrow's tears away,
Nor let me ever stray
  From Thee aside.

Hymn 244.   C. M

MY God, accept my heart this day,
  And make it always Thine,
That I from Thee no more may stray,
  No more from Thee decline.

2 Before the cross of Him who died,
  Behold, I prostrate fall;
Let every sin be crucified,
  Let Christ be all in all.

3 Anoint me with Thy heavenly grace,
  Adopt me for Thine own;
That I may see Thy glorious face,
  And worship at Thy throne.

4 May the dear blood once shed for me
  My blest atonement prove;
That I from first to last may be
  The purchase of Thy love!

c

5 Let every thought, and work, and word,
    To Thee be ever given;
Then life shall be Thy service, Lord,
    And death the gate of heaven!

THE LORD'S SUPPER.

Hymn 245.   P. M.

BREAD of the world, in mercy broken,
    Wine of the soul, in mercy shed,
By whom the words of life were spoken,
    And in whose death our sins are dead:

2 Look on the heart by sorrow broken,
    Look on the tears by sinners shed,
And be Thy feast to us the token
    That by Thy grace our souls are fed.

SUNDAY SCHOOLS.

Hymn 246.   C. M.

BY cool Siloam's shady rill
    How fair the lily grows!
How sweet the breath, beneath the hill,
    Of Sharon's dewy rose!

2 Lo, such the child, whose early feet
  The path of peace have trod,
Whose secret heart, with influence sweet,
  Is upward drawn to God.

3 By cool Siloam's shady rill
  The lily must decay;
The rose, that blooms beneath the hill,
  Must shortly fade away.

4 And soon, too soon, the wintry hour
  Of man's maturer age
Will shake the soul with sorrow's power,
  And stormy passion's rage.

5 O Thou, who givest life and breath,
  We seek Thy grace alone,
In childhood, manhood, age, and death,
  To keep us still Thine own.

FUNERALS.

Hymn 247. P. M.

THOU art gone to the grave! but we will
    not deplore thee,
  Though sorrow and darkness encompass
    the tomb;
Thy Saviour hath passed through its portals
    before thee,
  And the lamp of His love was thy guide
    through the gloom.

2 Thou art gone to the grave! we no longer
    behold thee,
    Nor tread the rough paths of the world
      by thy side;
  But the wide arms of mercy were spread to
    enfold thee,
    And sinners may die, for the Sinless hath
      died.

3 Thou art gone to the grave! and, its man-
    sion forsaking,
    Perhaps thy weak spirit in fear lingered
      long;
  But the mild rays of Paradise dawned on
    thy waking,
    And the sound which thou heard'st was
    the seraphim's song.

4 Thou art gone to the grave! but we will
    not deplore thee,
    Whose God was thy Ransom, thy Guar-
      dian and Guide:
  He gave thee, He took thee, and He will
    restore thee;
    And death hath no sting, for the Saviour
    hath died.

PRAYER.

Hymn 248.   III '.

COME, my soul, thy suit prepare,
  Jesus loves to answer prayer;
He Himself has bid thee pray,
Therefore will not say thee nay.

2 Thou art coming to a King,
  Large petitions with thee bring;
For His grace and power are such,
None can ever ask too much.

3 With my burden I begin;
  Lord, remove this load of sin;
Let Thy blood, for sinners spilt,
Set my conscience free from guilt.

4 Lord, I come to Thee for rest,
  Take possession of my breast;
There Thy blood-bought right maintain,
And without a rival reign.

5 While I am a pilgrim here,
  Let Thy love my spirit cheer;
As my Guide, my Guard, my Friend,
Lead me to my journey's end.

6 Show me what I have to do,
  Every hour my strength renew;
Let me live a life of faith,
Let me die Thy people's death.

  4

REPENTANCE.

Hymn 249.   III. 1.

DEPTH of mercy! can there be
  Mercy still reserved for me?
Can my God His wrath forbear?
Me, the chief of sinners, spare?

2 I have long withstood His grace;
Long provoked Him to His face;
Would not hearken to His calls;
Grieved Him by a thousand falls.

3 Kindled His relentings are;
Me He now delights to spare;
Now my Father's mercies move,
Justice lingers into love.

4 Lo! for me the Saviour stands;
Shows His wounds, and spreads His hands
God is Love! I know, I feel;
Jesus weeps, and loves me still.

FAITH.

Hymn 250.   P. M

JUST as I am, without one plea,
  But that Thy blood was shed for me,
And that Thou bidd'st me come to Thee,
    O Lamb of God, I come.

2 Just as I am, and waiting not
  To rid my soul of one dark blot,
  To Thee, whose blood can cleanse each spot,
      O Lamb of God, I come.

3 Just as I am, though tossed about
  With many a conflict, many a doubt,
  With fears within, and foes without,
      O Lamb of God, I come.

4 Just as I am—poor, wretched, blind—
  Sight, riches, healing of the mind,
  Yea, all I need, in Thee to find,
      O Lamb of God, I come.

5 Just as I am, Thou wilt receive,
  Wilt welcome, pardon, cleanse, relieve;
  Because Thy promise I believe,
      O Lamb of God, I come.

6 Just as I am, Thy love unknown
  Has broken every barrier down;
  Now to be Thine, yea, Thine alone,
      O Lamb of God, I come.

Hymn 251.   C M

FOREVER here my rest shall be,
    Close to Thy bleeding side;
This all my hope, and all my plea,
  "For me the Saviour died."

2 My dying Saviour and my **God,**
    Fountain for guilt and sin!
Sprinkle me ever with Thy blood,
    And cleanse and keep me clean.

3 Wash me, and make me thus Thine own;
    Wash me, and mine Thou art; ˙
Wash me, but not my feet alone,
    My hands, my head, my heart.

4 Th' atonement of Thy blood apply,
    Till faith to sight improve;
Till hope in full fruition die,
    And all my soul be love.

Hymn 252.   L. M

JESUS, Thy blood and righteousness
    My beauty are, my glorious dress;
Midst flaming worlds in these arrayed,
With joy shall I lift up my head.

2 When from the dust of death I rise
To take my mansion in the skies,
E'en then shall this be all my plea,
"Jesus hath lived and died for me."

3 This spotless robe the same appears
When ruined nature sinks in years;
No age can change its glorious hue;
The robe of Christ is ever new.

4 Oh! let the dead now hear Thy voice;
  Bid, Lord, Thy banished ones rejoice;
Our beauty this, our glorious dress,
Jesus, the Lord, our Righteousness.

LOVE.

Hymn 253.   C. M

JESUS! the very thought of Thee
  With sweetness fills my breast;
But sweeter far Thy face to see,
  And in Thy presence rest.

2 No voice can sing, no heart can frame,
  Nor can the memory find,
A sweeter sound than Jesus' name,
  The Saviour of mankind.

3 Oh, hope of every contrite heart,
  Oh, joy of all the meek,
To those who fall, how kind Thou art!
  How good to those who seek!

4 But what to those who find? Ah! this
  Nor tongue nor pen can show;
The love of Jesus, what it is
  None but His loved ones know.

4 *

5 Jesus! our only joy be Thou,
　　As Thou our prize wilt be;
Jesus! be Thou our glory now,
　　And through eternity.

Hymn 254. C. M

MY God, I love Thee, not because
　　I hope for heaven thereby;
Nor yet because, if I love not,
　　I must forever die.

2 But, O my Jesus, Thou didst me
　　Upon the cross embrace;
For me didst bear the nails and spear,
　　And manifold disgrace,

3 And griefs and torments numberless,
　　And sweat of agony,
E'en death itself; and all for one
　　Who was Thine enemy,

4 Then why, O blessed Jesus Christ!
　　Should I not love Thee well;
Not for the sake of winning heaven,
　　Or of escaping hell;

5 Not with the hope of gaining aught;
　　Not seeking a reward;
But, as Thyself hast loved me,
　　O ever loving Lord!

6 E'en so I love Thee, and will love,
    And in Thy praise will sing;
Solely because Thou art my God,
    And my eternal King.

Hymn 255.   C. M.

HOW sweet the name of Jesus sounds
    In a believer's ear!
It soothes his sorrows, heals his wounds,
    And drives away his fear.

2 It makes the wounded spirit whole,
    And calms the troubled breast;
'Tis manna to the hungry soul,
    And for the weary, rest.

3 Dear name! the rock on which I build,
    My shield and hiding place;
My never-failing treasury filled
    With boundless stores of grace.

4 By Thee my prayers acceptance gain,
    Although with sin defiled;
Satan accuses me in vain,
    And I am owned a child.

5 Jesus! my Shepherd, Guardian, Friend,
    My Prophet, Priest, and King,
My Lord, my Life, my Way, my End,
    Accept the praise I bring.

6 Weak is the effort of my heart,
  And cold my warmest thought;
But when I see Thee as Thou art,
  I'll praise Thee as I ought.

7 Till then, I would Thy love proclaim
  With every fleeting breath;
And may the music of Thy name
  Refresh my soul in death.

PRAISE.

Hymn 256.   III 3

LORD, Thy glory fills the heaven;
  Earth is with its fulness stored;
Unto Thee be glory given,
  Holy, holy, holy Lord!
Heaven is still with anthems ringing;
  Earth takes up the angel's cry,
"Holy, holy, holy," singing,
  "Lord of hosts, the Lord most High!"

2 Ever thus in God's high praises,
  Brethren, let our tongues unite,
While our thoughts His greatness raises,
  And our love His gifts excite.
With his seraph train before Him,
  With His holy church below,
Thus unite we to adore Him,
  Bid we thus our anthems flow.

3 Lord, Thy glory fills the heaven;
　　Earth is with its fulness stored;
Unto Thee be glory given,
　　Holy, holy, holy Lord!
Thus Thy glorious name confessing,
　　We adopt the angels' cry,
" Holy, holy, holy"—blessing
　　Thee, the Lord our God most High!

Hymn 257.　　L. M.

AWAKE, my soul, to joyful lays,
　And sing Thy great Redeemer's praise,
He justly claims a song from thee;
His loving-kindness, oh, how free!

2 He saw me ruined in the fall,
Yet loved me notwithstanding all;
He saved me from my lost estate;
His loving-kindness, oh, how great!

3 Though numerous hosts of mighty foes,
Though earth and hell my way oppose,
He safely leads my soul along;
His loving-kindness, oh, how strong!

4 When trouble, like a gloomy cloud,
Has gathered thick, and thundered loud,
He near my soul has always stood;
His loving-kindness, oh, how good!

5 Often I feel my sinful heart
Prone from my Saviour to depart,
But though I oft have Him forgot,
His loving-kindness changes not.

6 Soon shall I pass the gloomy vale,
Soon all my mortal powers must fail;
Oh, may my last expiring breath
His loving-kindness sing in death!

7 Then let me mount and soar away
To the bright world of endless day;
And sing, with rapture and surprise,
His loving-kindness in the skies.

Hymn 258. C. M.

ALL hail the power of Jesus' name!
Let angels prostrate fall,
Bring forth the royal diadem,
And crown Him—Lord of all.

2 Crown Him, ye martyrs of our God,
Who from the Altar call;
Extol the stem of Jesse's rod,
And crown Him—Lord of all.

3 Hail Him, the Heir of David's line,
Whom David, Lord did call;
The God incarnate! Man divine!
And crown Him—Lord of all.

4 Ye chosen seed of Israel's race,
Ye ransomed from the fall,
Hail Him who saves you by His grace,
And crown Him—Lord of all.

5 Sinners, whose love can ne'er forget.
   The wormwood and the gall,
Go, spread your trophies at His feet,
   And crown Him—Lord of all.

6 Let every kindred, every tribe
   On this terrestrial ball,
To Him all majesty ascribe,
   And crown Him—Lord of all.

Hymn 259.

THE strain upraise of joy and praise:
                Alleluia.
For the glory of their King,
Shall the ransomed people sing;
                Alleluia.
And the choirs that dwell on high
Shall re-echo through the sky
                Alleluia.
They in the rest of Paradise who dwell,
The blessed ones, with joy the chorus swell.
                Alleluia.

2 The planets beaming on their heavenly way,
The shining constellations, join and say,
                Alleluia.
Ye clouds that onward sweep,
Ye thunders echoing loud and deep,
Ye winds on pinions light,
Ye lightnings wildly bright,
In sweet consent unite
              Your Alleluia.

3 Ye floods and ocean billows,
    Ye storms and winter snow,
Ye days of cloudless beauty,
    Hoar frost and summer glow,
Ye groves that wave in spring,
And glorious forests, sing
                    Alleluia.
First let the birds, with painted plumage
    gay,
Exalt their great Creator's praise, and say
                    Alleluia.

4 Then let the beasts of earth, with varying
        strain,
    Join in creation's hymn and cry again,
                    Alleluia.
Here let the mountains thunder forth sono-
        rous   Alleluia.
Here let the valleys sing in gentler chorus
                    Alleluia.
Thou jubilant abyss of ocean cry,
                    Alleluia.
Ye tracts of earth and continents reply,
                    Alleluia.

5 To God who all creation made,
    The frequent hymn be duly paid,
                    Alleluia.
This is the strain, the eternal strain, the
        Lord Almighty loves,   Alleluia.
This is the song, the heavenly song, that
        Christ the King approves. Alleluia.

Therefore we sing, both heart and voice
    awaking,   Alleluia.
And children's voices echo, answer mak-
    ing,   Alleluia.
Now from all men be outpoured
Alleluia to the Lord:
With Alleluia evermore
The Son and Spirit we adore: ·
Praise be done to the Three in One!
    Alleluia! Alleluia! Alleluia! Amen.

PEACE.

Hymn 260.   C. M

OH for a heart to praise my God,
    A heart from sin set free!
A heart that always feels Thy blood,
    So freely spilt for me;

2 A heart resigned, submissive, meek,
    My great Redeemer's throne;
Where only Christ is heard to speak,
    Where Jesus reigns alone;

3 An humble, lowly, contrite heart,
    Believing, true and clean;
Which neither life nor death can part
    From Him that dwells within;

5   D

4 A heart in every thought renewed,
  And full of love divine,
Perfect, and right, and pure, and good,
  A copy, Lord, of Thine!

5 Thy nature, gracious Lord, impart;
  Come quickly from above;
Write Thy new name upon my heart,
  Thy new, best name of Love.

Hymn 261. C. M.

THERE is a fold whence none can stray,
  And pastures ever green,
Where sultry sun, or stormy day,
  Or night is never seen.

2 Far up the everlasting hills,
  In God's own light it lies;
His smile its vast dimension fills
  With joy that never dies.

3 One narrow vale, one darksome wave,
  Divides that land from this;
I have a Shepherd pledged to save,
  And bear me home to bliss.

4 Soon at His feet my soul will lie,
  In life's last struggling breath;
But I shall only seem to die,
  I shall not taste of death.

5 Far from this guilty world, to be
  Exempt from toil and strife;
To spend eternity with Thee,
  My Saviour, this is life!

Hymn 262. C. M.

O LORD, my best desire fulfil,
 And help me to resign
Life, health, and comfort to Thy will,
 And make Thy pleasure mine.

2 Why should I shrink at Thy command,
 Whose love forbids· my fears?
Or tremble at the gracious hand
 That wipes away my tears?

3 No, rather let me freely yield
 What most I prize to Thee,
Who never hast a good withheld,
 Or wilt withhold, from me.

4 Thy favour, all my journey through,
 Thou art engaged to grant;
What else I want, or think I do,
 'Tis better still to want.

5 Wisdom and mercy guide my way,
 Shall I resist them both?
The poor, blind creature of a day,
 And crushed before the moth!

6 But oh! my inward spirit cries,
 Still bind me to Thy sway!
Else the next cloud that veils the skies,
 Drives all these thoughts away.

Hymn 263.

MY Saviour, as Thou wilt!
    Oh, may Thy will be mine!
Into Thy hand of love
    I would my all resign.
Through sorrow or through joy,
    Conduct me as Thine own,
And help me still to say,
    My Lord, Thy will be done.

2 My Saviour, as Thou wilt!
    If needy here and poor,
Give me Thy people's bread,
    Their portion rich and sure.
The manna of Thy word
    Let my soul feed upon;
And if all else should fail,
    My Lord, Thy will be done!

3 My Saviour, as Thou wilt!
    Though seen through many a tear,
Let not my star of hope
    Grow dim or disappear.
Since Thou on earth hast wept
    And sorrowed oft alone,
If I must weep with Thee,
    My Lord, Thy will be done.

4 My Saviour, as Thou wilt!
    All shall be well for me:
Each changing future scene,
    I gladly trust with Thee.

Straight to my home above,
    I travel calmly on,
And sing in life or death,
    My Lord, Thy will be done!

DAILY DEVOTION.

Hymn 264.   II. 5.

ABIDE with me! fast falls the eventide,
    The darkness deepens; Lord, with me
      abide;
When other helpers fail, and comforts flee,
Help of the helpless, oh abide with me.

2 Swift to its close ebbs out life's little day;
Earth's joys grow dim, its glories pass away;
Change and decay on all around I see;
O Thou who changest not, abide with me.

3 I need Thy presence every passing hour;
What but Thy grace can foil the tempter's
    power?
Who like Thyself, my guide and stay can
    be?
Through cloud and sunshine, Lord, abide
    with me.

4 I fear no foe, with Thee at hand to bless;
Ills have no weight, and tears no bitterness.
Where is death's sting? where, grave, thy
    victory?
I triumph still, if Thou abide with me.

5 *

5 Hold Thou Thy cross before my closing
        eyes;
Shine through the gloom, and point me to
    the skies;
Heaven's morning breaks, and earth's vain
    shadows flee;
In life, in death, O Lord, abide with me.

Hymn 265.   L. M.

FORTH in Thy name, O Lord, I go,
    My daily labor to pursue;
Thee, only Thee, resolved to know,
    In all I think, or speak, or do.

2 Give me to bear Thy easy yoke,
    And every moment watch and pray;
And still to things eternal look,
    And hasten to that glorious day.

3 Fain would I still for Thee employ ,
    Whate'er Thy bounteous grace hath
        given;
Would run my course with even joy,
    And closely walk with Thee to heaven.

Hymn 266.   C. M.

FAR from the world, O Lord, I flee,
    From strife and tumult far;
From scenes where Satan wages still
    His most successful war.

2 The calm retreat, the silent shade,
    With prayer and praise agree;
And seem by Thy sweet bounty made
    For those that follow Thee.

3 There, if Thy Spirit touch the soul,
    And grace her mean abode,
Oh with what peace, and joy, and love,
    She communes with her God!

4 There, like the nightingale, she pours
    Her solitary lays,
Nor asks a witness of her song,
    Nor thirsts for human praise.

5 Author and Guardian of my life!
    Sweet source of life divine,
And—all harmonious names in one—
    My Saviour! Thou art mine.

6 What thanks I owe Thee, and what love,
    A boundless, endless store,
Shall echo through the realms above,
    When time shall be no more.

Hymn 267. P. M.

NEARER, my God, to Thee!
    Nearer to Thee!
E'en though it be a cross
    That raiseth me;
Still all my song shall be,
Nearer, my God, to Thee
    Nearer to Thee!

2 Though like a wanderer,
   Weary and lone,
Darkness comes over me,
   My rest a stone,
Yet in my dreams I'd be
Nearer, my God, to Thee,
   Nearer to Thee!

3 There let my way appear
   Steps unto heaven;
All that Thou sendest me
   In mercy given;
Angels to beckon me,
Nearer, my God, to Thee,
   Nearer to Thee!

4 Then, with my waking thoughts
   Bright with Thy praise,
Out of my stony griefs
   Altars I'll raise;
So by my woes to be,
Nearer, my God, to Thee,
   Nearer to Thee!

5 Or, if on joyful wing,
   Cleaving the sky,
Sun, moon, and stars forgot,
   Upward I fly;
Still all my song shall be
Nearer, my God, to Thee,
   Nearer to Thee!

Hymn 268. L. M.

SUN of my soul, Thou Saviour dear,
It is not night if Thou be near;
Oh, may no earth-born cloud arise
To hide Thee from Thy servant's eyes.

2 When the soft dews of kindly sleep
My wearied eye-lids gently steep,
Be my last thought how sweet to rest
For ever on my Saviour's breast.

3 Abide with me from morn till eve,
For without Thee I cannot live;
Abide with me when night is nigh,
For without Thee I dare not die.

4 If some poor wandering child of Thine
Have spurned to-day the voice divine,
Now, Lord, the gracious work begin;
Let him no more lie down in sin.

5 Watch by the sick; enrich the poor
With blessings from Thy boundless store;
Be every mourner's sleep to-night,
Like infant slumbers, pure and light.

6 Come near and bless us when we wake,
Ere through the world our way we take,
Till in the ocean of Thy love
We lose ourselves in heaven above.

DEATH.

Hymn 269. L. M.

ASLEEP in Jesus! blessed sleep!
From which none ever wakes to weep;
A calm and undisturbed repose,
Unbroken by the last of foes.

2 Asleep in Jesus! oh, how sweet,
To be for such a slumber meet;
With holy confidence to sing
That death has lost its painful sting.

3 Asleep in Jesus! peaceful rest!
Whose waking is supremely blest;
No fear, no woe shall dim that hour
That manifests the Saviour's power.

4 Asleep in Jesus! oh, for me
May such a blissful refuge be;
Securely shall my ashes lie,
Waiting the summons from on high.

5 Asleep in Jesus! far from thee
Thy kindred and their graves may be;
But there is still a blessed sleep,
From which none ever wakes to weep.

Hymn 270. S. M.

FOR ever with the Lord!
Amen, so let it be:
Life from the dead is in that word,
'Tis immortality.

2 Here in the body pent,
 Absent from Him I roam,
Yet nightly pitch my moving tent
 A day's march nearer home.

3 My Father's house on high,
 Home of my soul, how near
At times to faith's illumined eye
 The golden gates appear!

4 Ah, then my spirit faints
 To reach the land I love,
The bright inheritance of saints,
 Jerusalem above.

5 Yet clouds will intervene,
 And all my prospect flies;
Like Noah's dove, I flit between
 Rough seas and stormy skies.

6 Lord, bid the clouds depart,
 The winds and waters cease,
And sweetly o'er my gladdened heart
 Expand Thy bow of peace.

Hymn 271.   C. M

JERUSALEM, my happy home!
 Name ever dear to me!
When shall my labors have an end,
 In joy, and peace, and Thee!

2 Thy walls are made of precious stones,
 Thy bulwarks diamond-square,
Thy gates are all of orient pearl:
 O God! if I were there!

3 O my sweet home, Jerusalem!
   Thy joys when shall I see?
The King that sitteth on Thy throne
   In His felicity!

4 Thy gardens, and Thy goodly walks
   Continually are green,
Where grow such sweet and pleasant flowers
   As nowhere else are seen.

5 Right through Thy streets, with pleasing
      sound,
   The living waters flow,
And on the banks on either side,
   The trees of life do grow.

6 Those trees each month yield ripened fruit;
   For evermore they spring,
And all the nations of the earth
   To Thee their honours bring.

7 Oh, mother dear; Jerusalem,
   When shall I come to Thee?
When shall my sorrows have an end?
   Thy joys when shall I see?

Hymn 272. C. M

ON Jordan's stormy banks I stand,
   And cast a wishful eye
To Canaan's fair and happy land,
   Where my possessions lie.

2 Oh, the transporting, rapturous scene,
   That rises to my sight!
Sweet fields arrayed in living green,
   And rivers of delight!

3 O'er all those wide, extended plains
   Shines one eternal day;
There God the Son forever reigns,
   And scatters night away.

4 No chilling winds, nor poisonous breath,
   Can reach that healthful shore;
Sickness and sorrow, pain and death,
   Are felt and feared no more.

5 When shall I reach that happy place,
   And be forever blest?
When shall I see my Father's face,
   And in His bosom rest?

6 Filled with delight, my raptured soul
   Can here no longer stay;
Though Jordan's waves around me roll,
   Fearless I'd launch away.

JUDGMENT.

Hymn 273.   P. M

DAY of wrath! that day of mourning!
   See fulfilled the prophet's warning,
Heaven and earth in ashes burning!

2 Oh, what fear man's bosom rendeth,
  When from heaven the Judge descendeth,
  On whose sentence all dependeth!

3 Lo! the trumpet's wondrous swelling
  Peals through each sepulchral dwelling,
  All before the Throne compelling.

4 Death is struck, and nature quaking,
  All creation is awaking,
  To its Judge an answer making.

5 Lo, the book, exactly worded,
  Wherein all hath been recorded;
  Thence shall justice be awarded.

6 When the Judge His seat attaineth,
  And each hidden deed arraigneth,
  Nothing unavenged remaineth.

7 What shall I, frail man, be pleading?
  Who for me be interceding,
  When the just are mercy needing?

8 King of Majesty tremendous,
  Who dost free salvation send us,
  Fount of pity! then befriend us!

9 Think, kind Jesus, my salvation
  Cost Thy wondrous Incarnation;
  Leave me not to reprobation!

10 Faint and weary Thou hast sought me,
   On the cross of suffering bought me;
   Shall such grace in vain be brought me?

11 Righteous Judge! for sin's pollution
Grant Thy gift of absolution,
Ere that day of retribution.

12 Guilty, now I pour my moaning,
All my shame with anguish owning;
Spare, O God, Thy suppliant groaning!

13 Thou the harlot gav'st remission,
Heard'st the dying thief's petition;
Hopeless else were my condition.

14 Worthless are my prayers and sighing,
Yet, good Lord, in grace complying,
Rescue me from fires undying!

15 With Thy favored sheep, oh, place me!
Nor among the goats abase me;
But to Thy right hand upraise me.

16 While the wicked are confounded,
Doomed to flames of woe unbounded,
Call me, with Thy saints surrounded.

17 Bow my heart in meek submission,
Strewn with ashes of contrition;
Help me in my last condition.

18 Day of sorrows, day of weeping,
When in dust no longer sleeping,
Man awakes in Thy dread keeping!

19 To the rest Thou didst prepare him
By Thy Cross, O Christ, upbear him;
Spare, O God, in mercy spare him.

ETERNITY.

Hymn 274.

LET me not, Thou King Eternal,
  Enter hell's domain infernal!
Where is grieving, where is sadness,
Where is sorrow, where is madness,
Where despair is ever sighing,
Where the worm is never dying,
Where the shameless are astounded,
Where the guilty are confounded.

2 Me, may Zion welcome, saved;
Tranquil city, seat of David;
God its builder, light immortal;
Orient pearl each blazing portal;
Crystal gold its streets; the nation
Of the blest its population;
Living rock the walls that bound it,
Christ the guard that dwells around it.

3 With what joyous gratulations
Throng Thy gates the festive nations!
What the warmth of their embracing!
What the gems Thy walls enchasing!
Through that city's streets are wending,
Holy throngs, their anthems blending;
There may I, with myriads glorious,
Chant Thy praise in psalms victorious!

Hymn 275.

BRIEF life is here our portion,
　Brief sorrow, short-lived care;
The life that knows no ending,
　The tearless life is there.
Oh, happy retribution!
　Short toil, eternal rest;
For mortals and for sinners,
　A mansion with the blest.

2 And now we fight the battle,
　But then shall wear the crown
Of full and everlasting
　And passionless renown.
The morning shall awaken,
　The shadows pass away,
And each true-hearted servant
　Shall shine as doth the day.

3 Oh, sweet and blessed country!
　The home of God's elect;
Oh, sweet and blessed country,
　That eager hearts expect!
Jesus, in mercy bring us
　To that dear land of rest;
Who art with God the Father,
　And Spirit, ever blest.

Hymn 276.

JERUSALEM, the golden!
　With milk and honey blest;
Beneath thy contemplation
　Sink heart and voice opprest.

6 *　　　　　E

I know not, oh! I know not
　What joys await me there;
What radiancy of glory,
　What bliss beyond compare.

2 They stand, those halls of Zion,
　All jubilant with song,
And bright with many an angel,
　And all the martyr throng.
There is the throne of David,
　And there, from toil released,
The shout of them that triumph,
　The song of them that feast.

3 And they, who with their Leader,
　Have conquered in the fight;
Forever, and forever,
　Are clad in robes of white.
Oh, land that seest no sorrow!
　Oh, state that fear'st no strife!
Oh, royal land of flowers!
　·Oh, realm and home of life!

4 Oh, sweet and blessed country!
　The home of God's elect!
Oh, sweet and blessed country,
　That eager hearts expect!
Jesus, in mercy bring us
　To that dear land of rest;
Who art, with God the Father,
　And Spirit, ever blest.

Hymn 277.

FOR thee, oh dear, dear country,
  Mine eyes their vigils keep;
For very love, beholding
  Thy happy name, they weep.
The mention of thy glory
  Is unction to the breast,
And medicine in sickness,
  And love, and life, and rest.

2 Oh one, oh only mansion!
  Oh Paradise of joy!
Where tears are ever banished,
  And smiles have no alloy;
Thou hast no shores, fair ocean!
  Thou hast no time, bright day!
Dear fountain of refreshment
  To pilgrims far away.

3 Oh, sweet and blessed country,
  The home of God's elect!
Oh, sweet and blessed country,
  That eager hearts expect!
Jesus, in mercy bring us
  To that dear land of rest;
Who art, with God the Father,
  And Spirit, ever blest.

INDEX.

A SELECTION OF

ADDITIONAL HYMNS.

213.　　　　　　III. 3.

(Additional Hymns, No. 218.)

1. HARK! a thrilling voice is sounding ;
　　"Christ is nigh !" it seems to say,
　"Cast away the works of darkness,
　　O ye children of the day !"

2. Wakened by the solemn warning,
　　Let the earth-bound soul arise ;
　Christ, our Sun, all sloth dispelling,
　　Rises in the morning skies.

3. Lo ! the Lamb, so long expected,
　　Comes with pardon down from heaven ;
　Let us haste, in godly sorrow,
　　Through His blood to be forgiven.

4. So when next He comes with glory,
　　Wrapping all the earth in fear,
　May we by His love be shielded !
　　May He to forgive draw near !

214.　　　　　　C. M.

(Additional Hymns, No. 221.)

1. ONCE more, O Lord, Thy sign shall be
　　Upon the heavens displayed,
　And earth and its inhabitants
　　Be terribly afraid ;

For, not in weakness clad, Thou com'st,
Our woes, our sins to bear,
But girt with all Thy Father's might,
His judgment to declare.

2. The terrors of that awful day,
Oh! who can understand?
Or who abide, when Thou in wrath
Shalt lift Thy holy hand?
The earth shall quake, the sea shall roar,
The sun in heaven grow pale;
But Thou hast sworn, and wilt not change,
Thy faithful shall not fail.

3. Then grant us, Saviour, so to pass
Our time in trembling here,
That when upon the clouds of heaven
Thy glory shall appear,
Uplifting high our joyful heads,
In triumph we may rise,
And enter, with Thine angel train,
Thy palace in the skies.

215. L. M.

(Additional Hymns, No. 222.)

1. HOSANNA to the living Lord!
Hosanna to th' incarnate Word!
To Christ, Creator, Saviour, King,
Let earth, let heaven, Hosanna sing.

2. Hosanna, Lord! Thine angels cry;
Hosanna, Lord! Thy saints reply:
Above, beneath us, and around,
The dead and living swell the sound.

3. O Saviour! with protecting care,
Return to this, Thy house of prayer:
Assembled in Thy sacred name,
Here we Thy parting promise claim.

4. But chiefest in our cleansed breast,
   Eternal! bid Thy Spirit rest ;
   And make our secret soul to be
   A temple pure, and worthy Thee.

5. So, in the last and dreadful day,
   When earth and heaven shall melt away,
   Thy flock, redeemed from sinful stain,
   Shall swell the sound of praise again.

216.   III. 3.

(Additional Hymns, No. 223.)

1. HARK ! what mean those holy voices,
   Sweetly sounding through the skies ?
   Lo ! th' angelic host rejoices ;
   Heavenly hallelujahs rise.

2. Cherubs tell the wondrous story,
   Joyous seraphim reply,
   "Glory in the highest, glory !
   Glory be to God most high !

3. Peace on earth, good-will from Heaven,
   Reaching far as man is found ;
   Souls redeemed, and sins forgiven !
   Loud our grateful harps shall sound.

4. Christ is born, the great Anointed ;
   Heaven and earth His praises sing !
   Oh receive Whom God appointed,
   For your Prophet, Priest, and King. ·

5. Hasten, mortals, to adore Him ;
   Learn His name to magnify,
   Till in heaven ye sing before Him,
   Glory be to God most high !"

4

217.

9(Additional Hymns, No. 225.)

1. BRIGHTEST and best of the sons of the morning !
   Dawn on our darkness, and lend us thine aid !
   Star of the East, the horizon adorning,
   Guide where our infant Redeemer is laid.

2. Cold on His cradle the dew-drops are shining ;
   Low lies His head with the beasts of the stall :
   Angels adore Him in slumber reclining,
   Maker, and Monarch, and Saviour of all.

3. Say, shall we yield Him, in costly devotion,
   Odours of Edom, and offerings divine,
   Gems of the mountain, and pearls of the ocean,
   Myrrh from the forest, and gold from the mine ?

4. Vainly we offer each ample oblation,
   Vainly with gifts would His favor secure ;
   Richer, by far, is the heart's adoration,
   Dearer to God are the prayers of the poor.

5. Brightest and best of the sons of the morning !
   Dawn on our darkness, and lend us thine aid !
   Star of the East, the horizon adorning,
   Guide where our infant Redeemer is laid.

218. . III. 2.

(Additional Hymns, No. 230.)

1. GO to dark Gethsemane,
   Ye that feel the tempter's power,
   Your Redeemer's conflict see,
   Watch with Him one bitter hour ;
   Turn not from His griefs away,
   Learn of Jesus Christ to pray.

2. Follow to the judgment hall ;
    View the Lord of life arraigned*;
Oh, the wormwood and the gall ;
    Oh, the pangs His soul sustained !
Shun not suffering, shame, or loss ;
Learn of Him to bear the cross,

3. Calvary's mournful mountain climb ;
    There, adoring at His feet,
Mark the miracle of time,
    God's own sacrifice complete ;
"It is finished !"—hear Him cry ;
Learn of Jesus Christ to die.

219.   II. 6.

(Additional Hymns, No. 231.)

1. OH, sacred Head, now wounded !
    With grief and shame weighed down !
Oh, sacred Brow, surrounded
    With thorns, Thy only crown !
Oh, sacred Head, what glory,
    What bliss, till now was Thine !
Yet though despised and gory,
    I joy to call Thee mine.

2. On me, as Thou art dying,
    Oh turn Thy pitying eye !
To Thee for mercy crying,
    Before Thy cross I lie.
Thy grief and Thy compassion
    Were all for sinners' gain ;
Mine, mine was the transgression,
    But Thine the deadly pain.

3. What language shall I borrow
   To praise Thee, dearest Friend,
For this, Thy dying sorrow,
   Thy pity without end?
Oh, make me Thine forever,
   And should I fainting be,
Lord, let me never, never,
   Outlive my love to Thee.

4. Be near when I am dying ;
   Oh, show Thy cross to me !
And to my succor flying,
   Come, Lord, and set me free.
These eyes new faith receiving,
   From Thine eyes shall not move ;
For he who dies believing
   Dies safely through Thy love.

220.

(Additional Hymns, No. 233.)

1. JESUS Christ is risen to-day,
   Our triumphant holiday ;
   Who did once upon the cross
   Suffer to redeem our loss.
                    Hallelujah !

2. Hymns of praise then let us sing
   Unto Christ, our heavenly King ;
   Who endured the cross and grave,
   Sinners to redeem and save.
                    Hallelujah !

3. But the pains which He endured
   Our salvation have procured ;
   Now above the sky He's King,
   Where the angels ever sing,
                    Hallelujah !

221.

Veni Creator Spiritus.

1. Come Holy Ghost, our souls inspire,
   And lighten with celestial fire.
   Thou the anointing Spirit art,
   Who dost Thy seven-fold gifts impart.
   Thy blessed Unction from above,
   Is comfort, life, and fire of love.

2. Enable with perpetual light
   The dulness of our blinded sight.
   Anoint and cheer our soiled face
   With the abundance of Thy grace.
   Keep far our foes, give peace at home ;
   Where Thou art guide, no ill can come.

3. Teach us to know the Father, Son,
   And Thee, of both, to be but One.
   That, through the ages all along,
   This may be our endless song ;
       Praise to Thy eternal merit,
       Father, Son, and Holy Spirit.

222.   C. M.

(Additional Hymns, No. 238.)

1. SPIRIT of Truth ! on this Thy day
       To Thee for help we cry,
   To guide us through the dreary way
       Of dark mortality.

2. We ask not, Lord, the cloven flame
       Or tongues of various tone ;
   But long Thy praises to proclaim,
       With fervor in our own.

3. We mourn not that prophetic skill
    Is found on earth no more ;
  Enough for us to trace Thy will
    In Scripture's sacred lore.

4. Though tongues shall cease and power decay,
    And knowledge empty prove,
  Do Thou Thy trembling servants stay
    With faith, with hope, with love.

223.

(Additional Hymns, No. 240.)

1. THOU, whose Almighty word,
    Chaos and darkness heard,
      And took their flight !
  Hear us, we humbly pray.
  And where the gospel day
  Sheds not its glorious ray,
      Let there be light!

2. Thou who didst come to bring
    On Thy redeeming wing
      Healing and sight,
  Health to the sick in mind,
  Light to the spirit-blind,
  Oh, now to all mankind
      Let there be light !

3. Spirit of Truth and Love,
    Life-giving, holy Dove,
      Speed forth Thy flight !
  Move on the water's face,
  Spreading the beams of grace,
  And in earth's darkest place
      Let there be light !

4. Blessed and Holy Three,
   Glorious Trinity,
     Grace, Love, and Light!
   Through the world, far and wide,
   Boundless as ocean's tide
   Rolling in fullest pride,
     Let there be light!

224.

(Additional Hymns, No. 245.)

1. BREAD of the world, in mercy broken,
     Wine of the soul, in mercy shed,
   By Whom the words of life were spoken,
     And in Whose death our sins are dead :

2. Look on the heart by sorrow broken,
     Look on the tears by sinners shed,
   And be Thy feast to us the token
     That by Thy grace our souls are fed.

225.   C. M.

(Additional Hymns, No. 253.)

1. JESUS! the very thought of Thee
     With sweetness fills my breast ;
   But sweeter far Thy face to see,
     And in Thy presence rest.

2. No voice can sing, no heart can frame,
     Nor can the memory find,
   A sweeter sound than Jesus' name,
     The Saviour of mankind.

3. Oh, hope of every contrite heart,
     Oh, joy of all the meek,
   To those who fall, how kind Thou art !
     How good to those who seek !

4. But what to those who find ?   Ah ! this
    Nor tongue nor pen can show ;
The love of Jesus, what it is
    None but His loved ones know.

5. Jesus ! our only joy be Thou,
    As Thou our prize wilt be ;
Jesus ! be Thou our glory now,
    And through eternity.

226.   C. M.

(Additional Hymns, No. 254.)

1. MY God, I love Thee, not because
    I hope for heaven thereby ;
Nor yet because, if I love not,
    I must forever die.

2. But, O my Jesus, Thou didst me
    Upon the cross embrace ;
For me didst bear the nails and spear,
    And manifold disgrace.

3. And griefs and torments numberless,
    And sweat of agony,
E'en death itself ; and all for one
    Who was Thine enemy.

4. Then why, O blessed Jesus Christ !
    Should I not love Thee well ;
Not for the sake of winning heaven,
    Or of escaping hell ;

5. Not with the hope of gaining aught ;
    Not seeking a reward ;
But, as Thyself hast loved me,
    O ever loving Lord !

6. E'en so I love Thee, and will love,
    And in Thy praise will sing ;
Solely because Thou art my God,
    And my eternal King.

227.   III. 3.

(Additional Hymns, No. 256.)

1. LORD, Thy glory fills the heaven ;
   Earth is with its fulness stored ;
Unto Thee be glory given,
   Holy, holy, holy Lord ! ·
Heaven is still with anthems ringing ;
   Earth takes up the angels' cry,
"Holy, holy, holy," singing,
   "Lord of hosts, the Lord most High !"

2. Ever thus in God's high praises,
   Brethren, let our tongues unite,
While our thoughts His greatness raises,
   And our love His gifts excite.
With His seraph train before Him,
   With His holy church below,
Thus unite we to adore Him,
   Bid we thus our anthems flow.

3. Lord, Thy glory fills the heaven ;
   Earth is with its fulness stored ;
Unto Thee be glory given,
   Holy, holy, holy Lord !
Thus Thy glorious name confessing,
   We adopt the angels' cry,
"Holy, holy, holy"—blessing
   Thee, the Lord our God most High !

228.   II. 5.

(Additional Hymns, No. 264.)

1. ABIDE with me ! fast falls the eventide,
The darkness deepens ; Lord, with me abide ;
When other helpers fail, and comforts flee,
Help of the helpless, oh abide with me.

2. Swift to its close ebbs out life's little day ;
   Earth's joys grow dim, its glories pass away ;
   Change and decay on all around I see ;
   O Thou who changest not, abide with me.

3. I need Thy presence every passing hour ;
   What but Thy grace can foil the tempter's power ?
   Who like Thyself, my guide and stay can be ?
   Through cloud and sunshine, Lord, abide with me.

4. I fear no foe, with Thee at hand to bless ;
   Ills have no weight, and tears no bitterness.
   Where is death's sting ? where, grave, thy victory ?
   I triumph still, if Thou abide with me.

5. Hold Thou Thy cross before my closing eyes ;
   Shine through the gloom, and point me to the skies ;
   Heaven's morning breaks, and earth's vain shadows
       flee ;
   In life, in death, O Lord, abide with me.

229.

(Additional Hymns, No. 267.)

1. NEARER, my God, to Thee !
       Nearer to Thee !
   E'en though it be a cross
       That raiseth me ;
   Still all my song shall be,
   Nearer, my God, to Thee,
       Nearer to Thee !

2. Though like a wanderer,
       Weary and lone,
   Darkness comes over me,
       My rest a stone,
   Yet in my dreams I'd be
   Nearer, my God, to Thee,
       Nearer to Thee !

3. There let my way appear
   Steps unto heaven;
All that Thou sendest me
   In mercy given;
Angels to beckon me,
Nearer, my God, to Thee,
   Nearer to Thee!

4. Then, with my waking thoughts
   Bright with Thy praise,
Out of my stony griefs
   Altars I'll raise;
So by my woes to be,
Nearer, my God, to Thee,
   Nearer to Thee!

5. Or, if on joyful wing,
   Cleaving the sky,
Sun, moon, and stars forgot,
   Upward I fly;
Still all my song shall be,
Nearer, my God, to Thee,
   Nearer to Thee!

230.

(Additional Hymns, No. 268.)

1. SUN of my soul, Thou Saviour dear,
It is not night if Thou be near;
Oh, may no earth-born cloud arise
To hide Thee from Thy servant's eyes.

2. When the soft dews of kindly sleep,
My wearied eye-lids gently steep,
Be my last thought, how sweet to rest
For ever on my Saviour's breast.

3. Abide with me from morn till eve,
   For without Thee I cannot live ;
   Abide with me when night is nigh,
   For without Thee I dare not die.

4. If some poor wandering child of Thine
   Have spurned to-day the voice divine,
   Now, Lord, the gracious work begin ;
   Let him no more lie down in sin.

5. Watch by the sick ; enrich the poor
   With blessings from Thy boundless store ;
   Be every mourner's sleep to-night,
   Like infant slumbers, pure and light.

6. Come near and bless us when we wake,
   Ere through the world our way we take,
   Till in the ocean of Thy love
   We lose ourselves in heaven above.

231. II. 6.

(Additional Hymns, No. 275.)

1. BRIEF life is here our portion,
   Brief sorrow, short-lived care ;
   The life that knows no ending,
   The tearless life is there.
   Oh, happy retribution !
   Short toil, eternal rest ;
   For mortals and for sinners,
   A mansion with the blest.

2. And now we fight the battle,
   But then shall wear the crown
   Of full and everlasting
   And passionless renown.
   The morning shall awaken,
   The shadows pass away,
   And each true-hearted servant
   Shall shine as doth the day.

3. Oh, sweet and blessed country !
   The home of God's elect ;
Oh, sweet and blessed country,
   That eager hearts expect !
Jesus, in mercy bring us
   To that dear land of rest ;
Who art with God the Father,
   And Spirit, ever blest:

232.

II. 6.

(Additional Hymns, No. 276.)

1. JERUSALEM, the golden !
   With milk and honey blest ;
Beneath thy contemplation
   Sink heart and voice opprest.
I know not, oh ! I know not
   What joys await me there ;
What radiancy of glory,
   What bliss beyond compare.

2. They stand, those halls of Zion,
   All jubilant with song,
And bright with many an angel,
   And all the martyr throng.
There is the throne of David,
   And there, from toil released,
The shout of them that triumph,
   The song of them that feast.

3. And they, who with their Leader,
   Have conquered in the fight ;
Forever, and forever,
   Are clad in robes of white.
Oh, land that seest no sorrow !
   Oh, state that fear'st no strife !
Oh, royal land of flowers !
   Oh, realm and home of life !

4. Oh, sweet and blessed country !
   The home of God's elect !
Oh, sweet and blessed country,
   That eager hearts expect !
Jesus, in mercy bring us
   To that dear land of rest ;
Who art, with God the Father,
 · And Spirit, ever blest.

233.　　　　　　　　　　II. 6.
(Additional Hymns, No. 277.)

1. For thee, oh, dear, dear country,
   Mine eyes their vigils keep ;
For very love, beholding
   Thy happy name, they weep.
The mention of thy glory
   Is unction to the breast,
And medicine in sickness,
   And love, and life, and rest.

2. Oh one, oh only mansion !
   Oh Paradise of joy !
Where tears are ever banished,
   And smiles have no alloy ;
Thou hast no shores, fair ocean !
   Thou hast no time, bright day ;
Dear fountain of refreshment
   To pilgrims far away.

3. Oh, sweet and blessed country,
   The home of God's elect !
Oh, sweet and blessed country,
   That eager hearts expect !
Jesus, in mercy bring us
   To that dear land of rest ;
Who art, with God the Father,
   And Spirit, ever blest.

New York ; H. B. DURAND ; 11 Bible House.